A LARK UP THE NOSE OF TIME

Wayne F. burke

BareBackPress

This is a work of fiction. The characters, incidents, and dialogue are the products of the author's imagination and are not to be construed as real. Any resemblance to actual events or person, living or dead, is entirely coincidental.

BareBackPress
Hamilton, Ontario, Canada
For enquiries visit www.barebackpress.com
For information contact barebackpress@gmail.com
Cover layout and art: © Peter Jelen

No part of this can be used or reproduced in any manner whatsoever without written permission, except in the case of brief quotations embodied in critical articles and reviews. For information address BareBackPress.

COPYRIGHT © 2017 Wayne F. Burke
All RIGHTS RESERVED
ISBN-13: 978-1926449142
ISBN-10: 1926449142

POEMS

Fat Bastard - 1
Babies - 2
Disgust - 4
Bill - 5
Posse - 6
Ball Player - 7
Holy Moly - 8
Kamikaze - 9
Beach - 10
10 Cents - 11
Bomber - 12
Loony Bin - 13
Mr. Stain - 15
Sphincter - 16
Schwartzie - 18
The Joint - 21
Vane - 22
Trailways - 23
Pizza - 24
Oh Say Do You See - 25
Roach - 26
Lights - 27
Brad - 28
Tongue - 29
Nips - 30
Host - 31
Roy - 32
Quebec - 33
A Lark Up The Nose Of Time - 37
Scars - 39
Twilight - 40
Die - 41
Pumpkinseed - 42
Pain - 43

My Car, My Life - 44
House In Barre, Vermont - 45
Sonata No. 21 - 46
Fall - 47
Prayer - 48
Stars - 49
Mercy - 50
Bird - 51
Leave The Driftwood Motel - 55
At The Dinner Table - 56
My Jacket - 57
Walk With My Hands - 58
An Old Crow - 59
The Mean Girl Has - 60
What Kind Of Greeting - 61
2 Fagillahas On A Porch - 62
Waves Of High Tide - 63
Thump - 67
Herr Trumpf - 68
President Donald Trump - 69
He Ha - 70
How Do I Love Thee? - 73
Reasons - 74
Dumbfucks - 75
The Brown Chair - 76
Drink? - 77
Oasis - 78
22 North - 79
Future - 80
Straight - 81
Piels - 82
108 Mph - 83
Todd - 84
Feed - 85
Knock Knock - 86
Baby - 87

WFB - 88
Black Out - 89
Advice - 90
Lou (1954-2016) - 91
Spirit - 92

A LARK UP THE NOSE OF TIME

WAYNE F. BURKE

DEDICATED TO SHELIA O'GRADY, STEVEN GRANDE, AND COACH TIM CORKERY—TEACHERS, ALL.

DIRTY SUN

Fat Bastard

I sailed down the hillside
on my silver saucer
and when the saucer hit the road
I jumped up running
as long-legged Big Louie,
lanky and peanut-headed,
chased me;
his eyes squinted in a raisin-face
the white wall of my house down the street
bounced up and down
my rubberized clod-hopper boots
I ran up the drive
an ice-ball slammed into the side of my face
Big Louie screamed,
triumphant,
I ran up the frozen porch steps
bawling
and barged into the kitchen
where my Uncle,
home from work at the gas station,
stood before the stove
cooking:
"Big Louie hit me!" I shouted
then ducked
in case my Uncle tried to slap me
for interrupting his Saturday afternoon;
"get in the car," he growled
he came out of the house wearing his black Navy pea-coat
and looking like a mitten with a head,
we floated down the white street
snow banks to the push button-windows
of the big Buick Electra
to the skating rink
where Big Louie
his pals
stood in a phalanx
arms crossed on chests,
brave in a group,
like wolves--
my Uncle stepped up to them,
short

round
a svelte 320 pounds
a saturnine face
his leather hand shot out
and Louie fell down,
got up
his face
red like a stop sign
he ran
like a deer
loping strides up and over the snowbank
and into the tree line...
My Uncle got back into the car,
said "he won't call me
a 'fat bastard' again."

Babies

a priest from the big city
came to town
and spoke
at our confirmation
he was stout
with a broad beefy face
and pudgy hands that punched out
as he told us
that a kiss
by itself
was not a sin
but that "prolonged kissing" was
because
he said
it led to other sins
which
he suggested
we might well imagine
and I did
or tried to
ten years old
and concluded that
prolonged kissing was what
brought babies into the world
and so
when Chief Larson from the neighborhood
asked me if I knew how babies were made
I said "prolonged kissing"
and he laughed himself
silly
but I knew
that I was right
because the holy priest
had said so.

Disgust

we shoveled the snow off the line kiln
road
which iced-over
and we rode our sleds
sixty miles an hour
down
and out into a back street
where we took our chances
with cars
and one day
between the time it took me to hike
from bottom of the road
to top
a snow plow had come
and gone
and left a snow drift
that I hit
and went airborne
like a ski jumper
and I landed
on my sled
but my head out beyond
the steering bar
and I broke my front teeth
off
on the road
and got up
and ran home
each icy stinging breath
and burst into the warm steamy kitchen
and cried "I broke my teeth!"
and my grandmother turned to me
concernedly
but my sister gave me a look
of disgust
which
I hated her for.

Bill

stepped off of the town bus one day
and onto the field
where we played football
and told us his name was "Bill"
and that he had watched us
from the bus
and that
if we would let him
he would be our manager
and try and arrange games
between us and teams from
other towns...
He wore glasses and had a long
horse-face plus white shirt and
black slacks on a bowling-pin shaped
body;
he came by every day afterward
to watch us;
he said he would be our score-keeper
and that he would write stories about us
and have the stories published in the
newspaper...
At the dinner table my Uncle
asked about Bill
and I told him what Bill had said
he would do for us
and the next day my Uncle
showed up at the field
and told Bill to get lost and to stay
the hell away from us
and me and the other kids
did not know why my Uncle
was so upset or
why he had told Bill to go away
because,
we all agreed,
Bill was a nice guy
a very very nice guy.

Posse

in 5th grade I beat-up a 6th grader
in the schoolyard
and after school
the 6th grader and
a posse of his friends
chased me and a buddy
around
the neighborhood
until we were treed
like coons
on the roof of the
Farnham's garage
and Mr. Farnham,
with half a bag on,
screamed at us
to get down
and we did
and the 6th grader
started to beat on my buddy
and I went to his aid
and got beat on
by the rest
until
from the Farnham's block
3 girls ran out
and saved me
because,
they afterwards
said,
the fight was not fair:
none of us knowing
then
that
nothing is.

Ballplayer

I was twelve years old
and played baseball
all that summer at
a field by the lime kiln
where we gathered in
morning fog with all the
gloves and bats we owned.
Right field was waist-high
with picker bushes and
left ran downhill to the
Decensi's chicken coop;
rocks were bases and
the wire fence backstop was
put up by Chief's naunoo, Pete.
The kiln snorted and smoked,
cleared its throat and spat;
trucks big as garages, called
"Ukes," roared up and down
the right field line. Games were
stalled to look for the ball or
to argue calls, otherwise we
played straight through,
broke for lunch then for
supper, then played until we
could not see the ball or
each other.

Holy Moly

"some Catholics you kids are"
Grandma says
as she ushers us
out the door
Palm Sunday
"hurry!
You are going to be late!"
We walk without haste
to the car
my sister drives
to the church
we climb concrete steps
to the yawning mouth
to the holy water fount
the pew
the stations of the cross
my sister,
her soul black
as soot,
leaves as mass begins,
the priest sits on a throne,
his voice drones,
my brother falls asleep
and I punch him,
to save his soul,
and he wakes
but instead of
thanking me
whips me
across the face
with a palm
on the ride home.

Kamikaze

I stood at the crest of the hill
and screamed at
Tumbleweed Larson
moving like a pin-ball from the slot
face-down on his Kamikaze Speed Racer Sled
but he did not hear
and disappeared
under the car
and the car's right rear tire
went up then down
and I ran
to the roadside
where Tumbleweed lay
eyes shut
face Q-ball white
a trickle of blood from
his mouth
call an ambulance
someone said
call the cops
call a priest
"I never even seen him"
the driver said...
Snow fell thick as
a fleece;
a door of a house slammed-to
like a gun shot
"oh his poor mother!"
dusk closed in
the streetlight dully gleamed
like an eye
the mother slid as if
on skates
bare-headed and a shawl
she shouted to her son
who did not answer
only an ambulance
in the distance
replied.

Beach

a hot muggy day
no one to play with
all the kids gone
to the beach
Charlie Baguette told me I could go
with him
his family
I ran home for my suit
and when I returned
they'd already gone...
I climb the tree in the yard
and sit
hidden by leaves.
I pick my nose until it bleeds.
The sky turns milky-white
and I am glad,
maybe the Baguettes will be drowned
in the coming storm;
I climb down and lie in the
driveway on hot cinder
that feels like sand:
I hope I get run over.
I watch a bird
a speck
far above
until
it disappears.

10 cents

the ice cream truck plays
"Home on the Range"
and I run into the house
and ask Grandma
for a dime
but she says
a nickel is enough
and I say "ice cream costs 10 cents!"
and she frowns
and asks if I am trying to send her
to the Poor House
and I wait
as she pulls her change purse from the drawer
and the music plays outside
and as I pluck a coin from
her wrinkled palm
she asks if I think that
money grows on trees
but I do not respond
because I need
to run
to catch the truck
before it leaves.

Bomber

the big backyard tree
hard as iron
had soft smooth bark of shallow ridges
I ran my hand over
and pressed my cheek against...
It grew string bean-like pods
a foot long
with pillow feathers inside;
my Uncle said they were watermelon seeds
and I wondered was it a lie
like everything else he said?
Dinner plate-sized leaves hid me
as I sat
high up
in the "bomber's seat"
a branch thick as a tire
that wiggled when I jounced it
and from where
when I was upset
I dropped bombs
on people below--
one's who deserved it.

Loony Bin

Jimmy lived across the street from me
in an apartment with his
grandmother
we played together
with army men
in the driveway
and then Jimmy moved up-street
to live with his parents
in a new house
by a golf course
my grandfather drove me to his house
each Saturday
we played with an electric train set
listened to records
played baseball in the yard
one afternoon
after watching Big Time Wrestling on TV
we staged a wrestling match
in the cellar
and Jimmy started to beat the shit out of me
body slams and choke holds
he was year older
and heavier
I fought for my life
afraid he would murder me
he looked like a murderer
to me
he threw me around like a sack
and only stopped because
his mother opened the door
and called us upstairs for
a snack…
I never went back
after that
and was leery of him
though distantly friendly
in Junior High School
when his tall handsome father
dropped dead of heart attack
on the 7th green
and Jimmy was sent back to live with his relatives

because his beautiful mother
a schizophrenic
was in and out of the loony bin.

Mr. Stain

they bumped me from
B to A-division English
taught by a soft-spoken
prick who wore cardigan sweaters
and who spoke
a different language
than I did.
His name was Mr. Speck
or Spot
or
whatever
I can't remember
it does not matter
he is only a stain
on the soles of
my oxfords
now.

Sphincter

a dozen of us football players
were standing around
shooting the shit
when a small army of guys
from the next town,
our hated rivals,
arrived in cars
and walked down the road
their legs and torsos in silhouette
from headlights on the highway.
Everyone ran except me, Tank, and
Leno who went down under guys'
who piled-on like leaves;
I went to his rescue
got punched
and a guy bobbed and weaved
his head in moonlight
I swung
and the guy's knees
buckled
and when he came back up
I swung again and he dropped
onto the gravel road
that the sneaker-ed feet tore at
as the grunts and groans became
louder under the hot moon--
Tank knocked guys down like
they were bowling pins,
bodies littered the ground;
I struck out at
I did not know who
or whom...
The bubble light of a cop car
turned everyone's face
ghoulish-blue;
I ran
into the shadows
ashamed
because my sphincter muscle had given way
but glad too
because

I had always wondered
whether or not
I was a coward.

Schwartzie

I threw him a pass and
the ball hit him
in the head
he could not catch
all he could do was shoot
he'd spent a lifetime on the court
his father had built in their backyard
the only Jew
on the team
I asked him how he liked his gefilte fish
and he did not like that
or me;
during practice I blocked his
layups because
he could not jump
just shoot
all he could do
shoot the eyes out,
when we played an all-black high school
he played like a pro
a master of the shvartzers
but against the goyim
he did not have it
tended to choke
and everyone wondered why
I said because he was a Jew
and Jews were no good
I knew,
because
my grandmother had told me so.

RIPE BANDANNA

The Joint

so drunk I could barely stand,
Mahoney held me up
at the bus stop in Cheyenne
after dark
after the bars
with big elk and antelope heads
on the walls
their sightless stars of eyes
and some guy who
said hello
said he remembered me
from being inside the joint--
the bus driver said I could not board
Mahoney spoke silver words
to get us on
I fell asleep in the seat
my head fell on Mahoney's shoulder
he elbowed me
like a punch
and I straightened
awake
for a moment
then went back
into the blackness
and the cell in the joint
where
I had never been.

Vane

Mr. Gootay, from India
owned a funky restaurant
on the backside of Harvard Square
in Cambridge, Massachusetts
where I worked as fry cook
putting out breakfasts
and lunches
and sweating my hangovers
off
over a sizzling grill
that baked my brain
and made me thirsty again,
and one night after work
in a bar
in Central Square
where Harvard does not live,
I got the shit beat out of me,
and the next morning
I went to work wearing
mirror sunglasses and
band-aids on my face,
and Mr. Gootay asked
"what happened Vane?"
and I said "I walked into a door"
and Mr. Gootay
standing with hands behind his back
and wearing a short white jacket
that made him look like a doctor,
said "unbeLEAVEable!"

Trailways

I stood outside the bus station
one night
in Burlington, Vermont
after hitting the bars
which I had got thrown out of
one after the other
and I puked a geyser
of mustard-colored whatever
that splattered the sidewalk
and my shoe tops
and a bus driver
with a stricken look
asked me "you do that?"
and I said "no"
and at the door of the bus
he gave me some shit
about getting on
but I plowed up the steps
and went to the back
and sat and added to the general stench
until I got off an hour later
in Montpeculiar
the state capital.

Pizza
for Wayne Lucia

a sweltering day in
Vermont
like May
like New Orleans sultriness
the three of us
floating up Bourbon Street
looking for a bartender
named Rajah (Roger)
from Bassten (Boston)
whom we did not find
and we wound up at a campground
outside of the city
and laid out sleeping bags
on the ground
and passed-out
as the bugs bit down
and I got up and went back into the car
and so did Leno
but Louie was too fucked-up
and lay outside all night
and in the morning
his face looked like a pepperoni pizza
and I tried not to laugh
when I looked at him
but I did.

Oh Say Do You See

Mahoney and me
were tough-guy poets
and radicals on campus,
State College,
Mahoney cut people to
shreds with
caustic words
the faculty held a special meeting
how to shut Mahoney up?
They could not do it
Mahoney played politics
with administration
was on first-name basis with
Deans;
we became undesirables
who smoked pot openly
made fun of the jocks
and future Susie-Homemakers of
America,
one night we went to the
basketball game
and sat up high
in the bleachers
away from everyone else
when the national anthem began
everyone in the gymnasium stood and
turned to us
only ones not standing
and Mahoney began to giggle
as I became self-conscious
and did not realize until
end of the music that
we had sat
in front of
the American flag.

Roach

drove all night, 10 hours
central Florida, north
my two buddies passed-out
in the seats
the Volkswagen Beetle engine
humming
the black night
bugs hitting the windshield
like ping pong balls
I smoked a roach
the car began to float
the road a golden pathway
a Donna Summer song
on the radio
I felt like the only person
awake
in the world
in the land of the snake
and crocodile
on the radio
oh oh
the radio...
thick morning fog
three lane highway
a big green sign
a black guy
driving a motorcycle
beside us
shouts
"you white devils!"

WELCOME TO ATLANTA

Lights

We got stopped by cops
in a show of blue light
and a cop told my cousin
"step out of the car"
and made him walk a straight line
touch his toes
then his nose
and my cousin,
as shit-faced as he was,
somehow passed the tests
and we drove off
to the club
where we picked-up two girls
and then drove up to the mountain top
with them
and parked;
the wind howled around the car
non-stop
the lights of the town dully glowed
in the valley below;
my cousin and his girl went for a walk.
My girl had bow-legs
and a pigtail;
she unzipped my pants
then pulled hers off
then straddled me
as I lay back,
then she sat and guided me
inside of her and
then moved up and down
and lifted off
as I shot
and the wind wailed
and the car rocked
and down below the lights winked
on & off.

Brad

I worked as house painter
for Brad
who weighed 300 pounds
and was afraid to go
up the ladders;
I painted the world white
all summer
and got blasted on pot
with Brad
a stoner
who bought a 16 oz. hot chocolate
and a hot dog every morning
before lighting the first joint;
he told me that
he watched porno films sometimes
and asked what I thought of him
doing that
(not much)
he told me that his wife
took it up the ass
but only when she was drunk.
He could be a prick at work
sometimes but
was a decent sort
through lost.

Tongue

the dental hygienist tells me
I should brush my tongue as
well as my teeth
and when I look in the mirror
and stick out my tongue
I see a scar in the middle of it
from the day I bit into it
while playing football--
tackled while running
with my mouth open,
puncturing the thing;
I remember that someone asked
if I wanted a band-aid and
someone else laughed
and that I played until
the game ended
and I think
we lost
too.

Nips

my Uncle got me into the laborer's union
local number whatever
and I went to work for the Pipe-Fitter's
building a hydroelectric dam
in the boondocks
of forests
and hills
my cousin Tommy,
who wanted to be a State Trooper,
and me
stood around holding onto our shovels
like our dicks
and shooting the shit
until we were sick of each other;
back at the shop
I rifled through stacks of
Playboy magazines
like a sex fiend
and in the shack
where we ate
everyone shut-up whenever
Joe spoke
because Joe was a funny bastard
who's stories made us laugh
(some days we sat in silence
and listened to each other chew)
lunch was the best time of the day
besides quitting time
when my Uncle would stop the car at the store
and a six-pack would be bought
and Mike the Welder
who rode shotgun
would buy 3 nips
and finish them all
plus a beer
or two
before we dropped him off.

Host

an ocean of clouds
above
and nickel-sized sun,
and on my tongue
a host
that I try not to bite
because it would be the same
as biting the body of
Christ
stuck to the roof
of my mouth
like plaster of Paris
I do not dare touch
its a sin
and so
wait
uncomfortable
trying not to panic
as the thing
slowly wilts
and the soggy body
goes down my
throat
like a boat over the
falls.

Roy

was a so-called "carpenter"
and I his helper
and one day
driving to a job
he waved to a guy on the roadside
and I asked who the guy was
and Roy said "my older brother"
and after a mile or so
"he fucked me in the ass
when we were kids"
and I glanced over at him
and he kind of laughed
and I thought of what I should say
and after another mile
or so
"have you gone to counseling?"
and he turned and looked out the window
and after another mile
said
"no."

Quebec

the Schwartz brothers owned the
Sporting Goods store
where Grandma did business
even though they were Jews
and Jews were no good
because,
Grandma said,
they were not modest
(were not allowed on the beach
in Quebec where she lived as a girl
there was a big sign NO JEWS)
but the Schwartzie's sold good stuff
plus they liked Grandma because
she paid all her bills on time,
sent them out as soon as they arrived;
one of the brothers was dour as an undertaker
unsmiling with a blue closely shaven face
the other, bald one, made wise cracks out the side
of his mouth,
the side his cigar was not plugged into;
I liked the wise guy best
and did not care if he was Jew or what
I liked the smell of the leather of the ball gloves
and the rubber of the bicycle tires
and the fumes of the stogie too.

A LARK UP THE NOSE OF TIME

A Lark Up the Nose of Time

we left Kansas after
the bars closed,
Ron and Steve and me
in a station wagon
that I passed-out
in the back of
and woke
below a huge steel arch
high above
like a gate to heaven,
but it was Saint Louis
which we bombed through
all the way to Daytona
and got a motel room
on the beach
and sat indoors for three days
as
hurricane winds drove white sea horses
to shore and
branches of palm trees whirled
like broken helicopter blades...
On day four we got sun burned
and drunk
and I was so hungry
I punched-out the Plexi-glass
of a candy machine
and tried to eat a candy bar
older then Methuselah
and in the morning I woke
wet
from piss
in my bed
and
covered up the spot
and we drove back
out of money
out of smokes
and Ron got ugly
without his fix
and Steve
a born-again liar

told one whopper after
another
all the way to Ottawa.

Scars

I was back in my hometown
and met a guy
I knew
in a bar
I had not seen him in years
he asked me how
I got the scars
on my face
I did not know they were that
noticeable
I could have told him it was because
I had lived a little
but he would not have understood
because
he had never left town,
his face was as unmarked
and smooth
as it had been in High School
where we had been
children
together.

Twilight

she did not come to me
for love
but for help
because she was troubled
had some kind of daddy-problem
I think
said that she
felt "safe" with me
and I wondered why
and if it was a compliment.
She stayed a few days
then went away
after saying she would be back
soon
and I sat on the porch
and waited
a week of afternoons
on a street of third floor
walk-ups
and peaked roofs
and gloomy twilight's
and car headlights few
and far between.

Die

don't want to die
while watching a mystery movie
on TV
as the old lady calls 9-1-1
and before the ambulance comes;
want to die in a shoot-out
with cops or
crooks
don't matter which,
on the docks of
Marsailles
on a foggy night
beneath a streetlight
with a dame bending over me
bawling
saying "don't die!"
while she slips her hand
into my pocket
to feel for more than
my wallet.

Pumpkinseed

a nickel-sized sun
on the roof of the
building across the street
a block of shade
with a fish above
a pumpkinseed I tug
out of the weed-choked lake
it's sharp spiny fins
the hook stuck deep
the fish panting,
in pain,
my Uncle takes it from my hand
and beats the fish like a paddle
on the top of the picnic table
and throws it back
into the black water
where it floats
on its side
like a reminder
to those
who swallow
hook, line, and sinker.

Pain

I watch a girl punch another
twice in the face
at the edge of the park
and I shout "hey!"
and the punched girl runs
away, through traffic
and across the street
while the other girl exults
"I punched her twice in the face!"
I feel the punched-girl's pain
and I start to sink,
mentally.
Such is life, I think;
I did not create it
can not remake it,
best to forget about it:
the girl's pain is mine
only if I make it
so.

My Car, My Life

my car stalls in the road
and I pull it over
into a gas station
a big guy inside
wearing a gas station uniform
I tell him my car
but can't think of it's name
"like a Porsche"
he tells me to follow
and we go inside the garage
my car up on a lift
wooden scaffolding around it
guy on scaffolding says "transmission"
and the big guy hands me a bill for $6000
I ask about a trade-in deal
and Al, my old boss from
my old job in mental health,
shows me around the lot
but
I can't make-up my mind
and announce I will pay the six grand
and take my car back
and the gas station guys and
customers wildly cheer
my decision
which
I feel good about.

House in Barre, Vermont

my apartment in an
Edward Hopper house
on a hill
alone
alone
and so lifeless
and still;
cradled by a blue sky
of eternal
nothing;
telephone poles without
lines,
no people
no calls
a shriveled cloud
a dog
barking
somewhere in the
distance.

Sonata No. 21

an ambulance screams into
view;
trees with new green bud-dresses
wave;
cars and trucks carry-on as before
as ever
one after another;
the sky is silent
as always
nothing but blue to say;
the ridge line is
petrified; poor
trees,
can't run from the ax
only clothe themselves in
green disguise.
The grass, the grass endures
as the breeze
that once blew down walls
ruffles the buds
and leaves
as the crow flies above
but not nearly
as high as
the hawk.

Fall

trying to decide what to do with myself,
I sit
on a park bench
in the sunlight
to think
and I get caught
in whirlwinds
of yellow and rust-colored leaves
rushing from one side of the park
to the other
like a mob storming a Bastille
but then
lying down just as quickly,
spent
apparently,
until they get up
and renew the rush
only in a different direction
obviously confused
and
unruly;
a tornado of them whirls into the road
and is run through by a truck
and scattered;
they are a spiritual force
mainly
though make a clatter on the sidewalk
like tiny horses' hooves
scuttling
like the clouds
across the sky,
not sure where they are going
either.

Prayer

after my operation
when I was so sick
and could not get up
out of bed without
tremendous effort and
pain
I prayed as I lay
in the dark of my bedroom:
I prayed to my mother
and to my father
and to Theodore Dreiser
and they helped me
a little
I think,
but the pills helped
more.

Stars

a river of stars
and yellow headlights of cars
in-coming
red tail lights out-going
under the bridge;
so this is Hollywood,
wonder if I will be mugged
dust under my shoes
walking over the stars in the
sidewalk
back to my motel
and sleep
until
3 A.M.
woke by a bomb
an earthquake
a car
run head-on into the
motel wall below,
shouts and screams
a helicopter above
womp womp womp
a pencil-thin beam of light
through the parking lot
this is not
Hollywood
it is LA
big city of broken dreams
and arms,
the chopper lifts off
into the dark
where stars of the milky way
shine brighter
than any on earth
ever did.

Mercy

overnight, the green backyard
below the window
has become a sea of white
flowing up against the shore
of fence;
I can hear the hiss
and almost see the wallow
as foam-white
crisps
surge
at the mercy of the waves
as we
at mercy of an Arctic front
watch from
cliff-top windows
of our heated huts.

Bird

sitting in the park
after dark,
thoughts of crude sex
in my head;
I spread my legs
and wait for her
to come
and sit
beside me
"squeeze my nuts" I say
and she smiles
"you can do it"
and
she does
and then my cock
her little hand
plump and
soft as a bird
she knows her stuff
she does
it is too cold
though
to take it out
and besides
there are cameras
watching.

HAIKU-YOU!

leave the driftwood motel
and head somewhere
up the coast

at the dinner table
my sister threatens suicide:
pot roast again

my jacket--
hung by the neck
until Spring

walk with my hands
in my pockets
among the descendants of the Mayflower

an old crow
in the parking lot
welcomes me to the nursing home

the mean girl has
cannonballs
strapped to her chest

what kind of greeting
is that?
The cold tongue of a dog.

2 fagillahs on the porch
one tall, one short
numbers 1 & 2

waves of high tide
crash into the balcony
and sleep

POLITICS, POLITICS.....

Thump

a loud THUMP on the door of
liberty
has splintered the wood,
shattered the glass;
the barbarians are at the gate:
the alarm sent too late,
Alaric in the driver's seat
and boots tramping on varnished floors,
heels ground,
drums beat...
A seismic shift and
spin and axis altered--
a redneck win,
hick victory
evangelical triumph--
the looting of the shrines begins--
the Know Nothings, disavowed by the Republic
in the 19th Century,
have arisen from the dead
and the country trembles.

Herr Trumpf

the redneck loudmouth hicks
and the bigots
have elected one of their own,
an orange-tinted diabolical businessman
who loathes his own constituents
and is using the dumb-fucks
to gain power
in order
to glorify his ego
that there is not glory enough
to ever come close to filling--
the know-nothings mumble trumpf
trumpf trumpf
as unsavory brown shirt-types tramp
tramp tramping mud
on the White House carpets...
The Statue of Liberty has sunk
into the harbor
and the Liberty Bell, already cracked,
has fallen to pieces.

President Donald Trump

I read the words in the newspaper
and realized
it is true and
not a bizarre dream:
my fellow citizens
in a fit of delirium
had voted Trumpian;
the orange-haired Wonderkind
with the crass style
will sit with Roosevelt
and Lincoln
inside the oval office...
What was unthinkable has been thought.
What seemed unbelievable has been brought
to be:
is it some kind of joke?
If so,
an unfunny one
with a punchline yet to be
delivered.

He Ha

remember when Trump was a joke
and everyone was laughing at him
and Hillary had that big smile
plastered to her face
during the debates?
That smile that let us, the viewers, know
that she knew Trump was a joke
and that she knew that we knew
he was a joke
and that she knew that we knew that she knew
he was a joke?
The fat lady has sung
and no one is laughing now,
least of all, Hillary.
Least of all
me.

SPARE TOOTH

How Did I Love Thee?

Let me count the swizzle sticks
and empty bottles
the cocktail shakers
and the olives
the coasters I never used
the glasses I did not bother with
the ice cubes I never wanted
the puddles on the bar
the soggy dollars
the hours
the hours
the stools and chairs
the jukebox
R 7 "Riders On the Storm"
A 4 "Sixteen Tons" by Tennessee Ernie Ford
the ashtrays
the smoking cigarette butts
the pickled eggs and crackers
the Slim Jims
the beer nuts...
I loved you more than the summer days
I glimpsed through
the curtained windows.

Reasons

motel sign like an illuminated
spark plug or
robot that
turns it's head to
look at me
lying on a bed
too hot
to sleep in
no air conditioning
this $65 a night box;
the night drips drop by drop
like sweat from
the ceiling:
I list the reasons
I do not like life
then I fall asleep
and when I wake
take them all back.

Dumbfucks

stationary bicycles go
nowhere
like me
except one year
my boss at work
threw me the key to his cottage
on Martha's Vineyard
and I drove down from Vermont
and crossed over on the ferry
to the island
which was mostly deserted
it was Thanksgiving
and cold
my first night there
I went out jogging and
could not find my way back
because all the cottages looked alike
a world of gingerbread houses
I felt trapped
like in a nightmare
and ran round and round
no one to ask directions
and on the verge of tears...
Afterwards, I took a cab
whenever I went out
the same cab same driver
we became friendly
after he realized I was no
rich tourist jerk
but a dumb-fuck like himself
he drove us down to the shore
where we watched a gull
rise up with a clam in its mouth
and drop the clam
on rocks below
until it broke--
it was one of the highlights of
my trip.

The Brown Chair

my ass sinks to the floor in this chair
I have sat in for years,
slept in for weeks,
a horrible brown and stained affair
worth $10 at a lawn sale
maybe less
but priceless to me
I miss it when I am gone too long
too busy to sit;
I have gone to Africa in this chair
have fought the 2nd World War over again in this chair
tried to have sex with a girl in this chair;
I wonder if I will die in this chair;
should probably get up and
out of this chair,
go and sit somewhere else
or stand
maybe walk around
go somewhere I cannot get to
by chair--
but where is that?

Drink?

A drink was always the
answer to
whatever problem:
toothache
heartache
debt
bad childhood
angst
"have a drink, you will feel better"
loneliness
hopelessness
frigidity
morbidity
headache
gout
"have a shot, it will help you out"
myocardial infarction
bankruptcy
old age
doubt
distress
PMS
"have a drink, it will fix you up."
Always.

Oasis

fading-blue sky and
banana-moon;
night coming on
like a mother and
me with nothing to do;
a girl I once knew,
what is her apartment number?
Will she be glad to see me?
I don't know;
the stars are clueless too;
lone pine trees above the ridge line
like arboreal heroes of some kind;
blood red stop lights turn
neon green
then wan yellow
the color of the Shell station
on the corner--
fake oasis
of the night.

22 North

driving up the Northway out of Albany
New York
in the distance
an ocean with
shoreline,
inlet,
great gray sea
above dark cloud base--
red tail lights of cars
moving in tandem along
3 lanes,
white headlights burst
into play around distant exit;
I drive up 22N
alone
the only car on the road
N
to Vermont cow fields
Big Dipper hung in the black sky
of diamonds
the car (BMW)
eating up the road
as the night unscrolls
before me.

Future

no future in lying around my apartment
playing with my dick
so I get up
go out
to crows croaking
who knows what
and bikers
destroying serenity wherever
they go
and cars with opened windows
driver's sharing their horrible
tastes in music,
and punks in hot rods leaving
streaks of testosterone on the
road
and my dick
and my future
both on hold.

Straight

the Italian stone cutter
30 feet high
in his element
in Dente's Park
after dark
warm Spring air
crossroads leading right,
left, back, and
straight up
the freeway
seems best to me
but unfeasible
at this time
unless I were out to ruin
my life
which
I am not
I am just in a bad place
feeling apart
red green white lights
gas station on the corner
OPEN
the stone cutter is looking
up the freeway too.

Piels

my beer was Piel's Real Big-Mouth
Draft
the bottles shaped like hand grenades
the opening a half-dollar sized
hole
like a little pond
I could take a dip in
to cool off
or swim across
or float on my back
but it always seemed
that
by the end of the night
I was face down.

108 mph

driving down the Interstate
at one hundred eight in
my BMW
wishing I were not alone
that there were someone else
like a bunch of kids
nephews and nieces
one of whom
would ask how fast
and I would say
"one hundred eight"
and all the kids are happy
as shit
because they never went 108 before
and when they get home
tell their parents
and the parents say
"isn't that wonderful"
and then the parents ask
the kids to leave the room
so that they, the parents
can speak to Uncle Wayne
in private.

Todd

had had a couple of drinks
maybe more,
and was driving his car down
a dirt road,
going to do some hunting,
when he saw
on the roadside
the biggest pheasant
he had ever seen
and he pulled the car over
and loaded his rifle
trembling with excitement
he stuck the barrel out
the window, aimed, fired
Blam!
A couple feathers flew up
and Todd thought
"what the fuck?"
then he heard banging on
the car's trunk
as a big game warden
shouted "drop the gun!"
and Todd put the rifle
aside
as the bird
stood there
staring
like a goddamn dummy.

Feed

on nights she forgets to feed me
I go into her bedroom
and slap her face
until she awakes
some nights even after she wakes
she rolls over
and goes back to sleep
on those nights I head-butt her
until she gets up,
the dirty slut.
Some nights, though awake
she falls asleep again at the table
in which case
I rub my parts against her
and give her little licks
and if that does not do the trick
I bite the bitch
which usually works
gets her moving to put
food on a plate
and the plate on the floor
where I can reach it,
and then the lovely girl
returns to bed
where I will join her
later.

Knock Knock

who is there?
A woman
says she has seen me around
and would like to get to know me
and can she come in?
I kick aside some books
and clothes so that
she can sit;
I play a record for her
on the gramophone.
If I had a gramophone--
if I had a record...
Hello?
Oh no, it is the landlord.
No it is the landlord's brother
my friend
whose friendship I need
like I need a hole put into my head;
I let him in
he says he wants to inspect the light fixtures
but
there are none
and I do not know what
happened to them
either.
The poor guy,
he begins to mutter,
but hey,
I cannot be expected to keep track of
everything
can I?

Baby

they yanked me out
with forceps,
9 lbs. 10 oz.'s
my beautiful mother
I hope she did not suffer
too much,
they say I slept through the nights,
say I was the "family entertainer"
with antics in my high chair and crib,
say I stood
a toddler
with my face pressed against the screen door
held my nose
and said "phew!"
each time a truck
drove past the house.

WFB

living with my curtains drawn
and my windows shut
to keep the neighbors out
of my life.
They shout at me wherever
I go out
but I do not respond
because
they're motherfuckers
trying to get me down,
but I won't let them,
won't allow it;
I'll live my life like a clam
behind curtains and
windows
until they come to me
one by one
and ask
"are you Wayne Burke
who writes poetry?"
and I'll say "yes,
yes, but to all you
suckers
it is 'Wayne F.'"

Black-Out

I wrote letters from
my rooming house
room while I was
blacked-out; a few
good ones, spare
and close to the bone;
most gibberish, some
illegible;
never sent them,
wonder where they are.
Long gone, like the
typewriter I used to
write them, like the
friends I wrote to,
like the person who
wrote them.

Advice

burn all bridges
as soon as you cross
them
because you are going to
want to
go back,
and if the bridge
is still intact,
you will.

Believe me,
you will.

Lou (1954-2016)

was a high hurdles man in High School
and a 130-pound safety on the football team
who did not always make the tackle
but was always head-first in the pile,
not a fighter
but would throw himself into the mix
heedlessly
and give of himself too
(and money whenever he had it)
he knew the words
girls' listen to,
had a wife, for awhile
and a kid, always;
had a brother who
took him in when he
was homeless;
he liked his sauce
(who doesn't?)
a six-pack in the morning
before work,
he never stayed sober for long
and he died head-first
the way he lived
not always making the tackle
but always the attempt.

Spirit

the spirit flew in
through the window
and down my
gullet:
I love it,
it tells me
that there is hope
that there is a future--
but the night, I said to the spirit
it is so dark,
and I am all alone;
and the spirit said that
it knows all about
the dark and
the lone,
and does not think much
of either.

ACKNOWLEDGEMENTS

I would like to gratefully acknowledge the following publications where some of these poems first appeared: Meat For Tea, Thirteen Myna Birds, Black Ink, The Rat's Ass Review, Your One Last Phone Call, Burnside Review, Bareback Anthology, Torrid Literature, Scarlet Leaf Review, Zombie Logic Review, Haikuniverse, Bear Creek Haiku, Almost Haiku, In Between Hangovers, Ink In Thirds, Clockwise Cat, Peeking Cat Review, The Stray Branch, Versewrights, The Bees Are Dead, 63 Channels,and the Loch Raven Review.

ABOUT THE AUTHOR:

Wayne F. Burke was born in 1954 to Claire Burke neé Kelly and Edward W. Burke. He was raised in the home of his paternal grandparents, as were his three siblings. His grandfather was owner and operator of BURKE'S INN, a generational business begun previous to the First World War. Wayne F. Burke attended public schools, and after High School, three institutions of higher learning before graduating from Goddard College in 1979 (B.A., RUP). After graduation he lived in a variety of places while working at a variety of occupations. In the mid-80's he located himself in the central Vermont area (USA) and has remained since. His first poetry collection (*Words That Burn*) was published when he was fifty-eight. Since then, three more collections have followed: *Dickhead, Knuckle Sandwiches,* and *A Lark Up The Nose Of Time*. A fifth volume, tentatively titled *Poems From The Planet Crouton,* is currently in progress.

ALSO BY THE AUTHOR

Words That Burn

Dickhead

Knuckle Sandwiches

Paddy Wagon

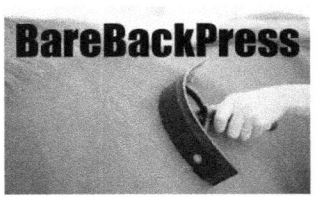

Also from BareBackPress

Better Than God
Peter Jelen

Euthanasia is a firing squad, the Catholic Church brings the Son of Man back to life with the Shroud of Turin, doctors create imaginary mental disorders to further their careers, and God hands in his letter of resignation in the form of a suicide note while lonely young girls seek out pedophiles on the Internet just for some attention.

Better Than God is a collection of dark and humorous fast-paced imaginative stories filled with unforgettable characters only Peter Jelen can provide.

Better Than God
$12.99
6" x 9"
254 pages
ISBN-13: 978-0988075016
ISBN-10: 0988075016
BISAC: Fiction / Short Stories

Knuckle Sandwiches
Wayne F. Burke

Knuckle Sandwiches is a punch in the face to art, culture, and society. A smack in the mouth to propriety. Knuckle sandwiches of the literal kind as well as the more common, but no less painful, metaphorical kind, which life gives to everyone regardless of race, creed, class, or gender.

Knuckle Sandwiches
$14.98
5.25" x 8"
116 pages
ISBN-13: 978-1926449081
ISBN-10: 1926449088
BISAC: Poetry / General

garbageflower
Damon Ferrell Marbut

With garbageflower, Damon Ferrell Marbut demonstrates once again how each book is its own unique expression of human engagement. The generosity of this collection comes from the shared moment, wherein often Marbut leaves defining the poem's purpose up to the reader. Other times there is no doubting how firmly he believes there is no line separating abstraction from reality. This believable, touching book of poems is for everyone.

garbageflower
$15.00
5.5 x 8.5
102 pages
ISBN-13: 978-1926449074
ISBN-10: 192644907X
BISAC: Poetry / General

Heaven's Gone To Hell
Andrew J. Simpson

Heaven's Gone To Hell leads the reader through a series of humorous dystopias that challenge the way we use language and the way we see the world. From alcoholic archangels, to heaven's reliance on unpaid labour, to a devil just trying to do what's right, Andrew J. Simpson's follow-up to The Big Picture turns the tropes of society on their ears.

"The mind of Andrew J. Simpson is an ideas machine … His brain is actually a powerful alien computer."

~ *Alejandro Bustos, Apartment 613*

Heaven's Gone To Hell
$19.99
6" x 9"
174 pages
ISBN-13: 978-1926449067
ISBN-10: 1926449061
BISAC: Fiction/ General

Remote Life
Edward Anki

Remote Life slices into the reader's mind like a paper cut, provoking thought, mild discomfort, and the unsettling thrill of a direct and immediate experience of reality. In this collection of poems, Edward Anki addresses the disconnectedness of modern urban existence in raw and unforgiving terms, offering an unfiltered take on everything from the struggles of dating to the stark actualities of aging and death.

Remote Life
$10.00
5.25" x 8"
46 pages
ISBN-13: 978-1926449029
ISBN-10: 1926449029
BISAC: Poetry / General

Impressions Of An Expatriate: China
Peter Jelen

Impressions Of An Expatriate is an honest, firsthand examination of one expat's experiences living in China dealing with culture shock, racism, and assimilation. From his encounters with children grown in cages to bears fighting to the death in a pit at the base of the Great Wall, Jelen's poems leave little to the imagination with haunting, vivid portraits that will take you on a trip.

"Jelen observes everything going on all around him, and as he sees it happening, he's taking it in, and becoming wise in the ways of the world…"

~ *Carl Miller Daniels*

Impressions Of An Expatriate: China
$8.50
5.25" x 8"5
60 pages
ISBN-13: 978-0992035563
ISBN-10: 0992035562
BISAC: Poetry / General

Hearing Voices
The BareBack Anthology

Since 2012 BareBack has sought to publish writers who are straightforward, sincere, and passionate. Hearing Voices: The BareBack Anthology features the most innovative and honest poetry, fiction, and flash fiction that has appeared in BareBackMagazine since its inception. Hearing Voices is bold, brave, and a great showcase of some amazingly talented new and established writers from around the world.

Hearing Voices: The BareBack Anthology
$14.99
6" x 9"
132 pages
ISBN-13: 978-0992035549
ISBN-10: 0992035546
BISAC: Poetry / General

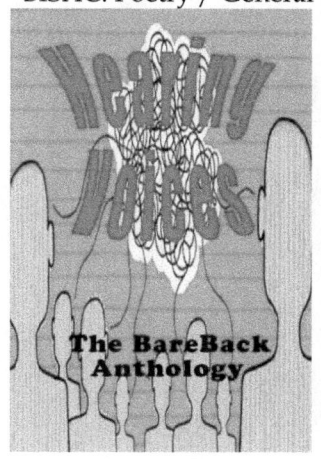

And So On...
The BareBack Anthology

A collection of innovative poetry from poets speckled around the world who have been featured in BareBack Magazine ~ an online publication dedicated to BareBack writers. People who aren't afraid to take off their gloves and give the world sincere, unpretentious, honest writing that has punch. *And So On...* is dark, humorous, and sometimes downright strange.

And So On...: The BareBack Anthology
$17.99
5.25" x 8"
134 pages
ISBN-13: 978-192-644-910-4
ISBN-10: 192-644-910-X
BISAC: Poetry / General

Be Kind to Strangers
Carl Miller Daniels

A wild and wondrous group of poems, BE KIND TO STRANGERS is the most recent collection of work by Carl Miller Daniels. Sweet, sexy, and alarming, with more than a hint of gentle absurdism, these poems cross the paths from sadness to joy, with a sense of awe and amazement that things in this world, are like they are.

Be Kind to Strangers
$8.50
5.25" x 8"
56 pages
ISBN-13: 978-1926449043
ISBN-10: 1926449045
BISAC: Poetry / General

DICKHEAD
Wayne F. Burke

One of the best volumes of poetry published this year or any year, DICKHEAD is an absurdist knuckle sandwich that deals in realism and farce in equal measures: simultaneously a punch to the gut and massage--jasmine mixed with hemlock--a ride through the Tunnel of Love and into the Fun House...An eclectic stew of poetry that engages both soul and spleen, heart as well as mind.

Dickhead
$13.00
5.25" x 8"
108 pages
ISBN-13: 978-1926449050
ISBN-10: 1926449053
BISAC: Poetry / General

Sedimentary Iguana-Land
Carl Miller Daniels

Sedimentary Iguana-Land, a new book by Carl Miller Daniels. The book consists of rants, musings, lists, poems -- and yes secret forbidden thoughts -- all of which Daniels had scrawled onto 3x5 cards over a period of many years, put into a dusty cardboard box, and kept there in that box, until he said what the heck, and decided to dig them out. Sedimentary Iguana-Land ~ ya ain't seen nothin' like it.

Sedimentary Iguana-Land
$8.50
5.25" x 8"
114 pages
ISBN-13: 978-1926449128
ISBN-10: 1926449126
BISAC: Poetry / General

The Human Condition Is A Terminal Illness
Matthew J. Hall

To be human is to come to terms with a repetitive and trying history; an acceptance of the potential beauty and the overiding toxicity of mankind. The Human Condition is a Terminal Illness, pulls individual and societal insecurities out from our collective subconscious in an effort toward analysis and question. More often than not, in the midst of a confused, selfish, self-hating populace, the answers are left wanting.

> The Human Condition Is A Terminal Illness
> $12.50
> 5.25" x 8"
> 140 pages
> ISBN-13: 978-1926449111
> ISBN-10: 1926449118
> BISAC: Poetry / General

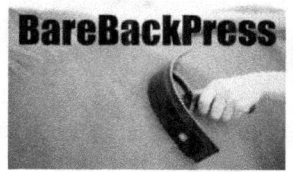

www.barebackpress.com
Hamilton, Canada

www.ingramcontent.com/pod-product-compliance
Lightning Source LLC
Chambersburg PA
CBHW060328050426
42449CB00011B/2693